COVET
TO
Prophesy

COVET
TO
Prophesy

ACTIVATING THE
PROPHETIC **DNA** IN YOU

DELON AARON
FOREWORD BY APOSTLE JAMES DUNCAN

Reviewers may quote brief passages in reviews.
Walton Publishing House
Houston, Texas
www.waltonpublishinghouse.com
Printed in the United States of America

Disclaimer: The advice found within may not be suitable for every individual. This work is purchased with the understanding that neither the author nor the publisher is held responsible for any results. Neither author nor publisher assumes responsibility for errors, omissions, or contrary interpretations of the subject matter herein. Any perceived disparagement of an individual or organization is a misinterpretation.

Brand and product names mentioned are trademarks that belong solely to their respective owners. Unless otherwise indicated, all Scripture is taken from the King James Version (KJV) of the Holy Bible.

Edited by: Omeyana Hamilton-Dummett and Jarienn A. James.
Cover designed by: Exponential Innovations by Harrison Forde

Library of Congress Cataloging-in-Publication Data under

ISBN: 978-1-953993-67-0

DEDICATION

To my praying mom Claire Aaron whom God used like Jesus' mom Mary who discerned His time when He performed His first miracle at a wedding when He turned water into wine. You sensed the time was ripe and introduced me to my first prophetic encounter where I was awakened to an anointing I never knew was resident inside of me, and ever since, the trajectory of my life has changed.

I also dedicate this book to my Help meet, my Rib, and my GOOD Thing, Ilene Aaron. Thank you for your enduring love, believing in me, and praying the vision through. To my sons, Zachary and Zion, you are the center of my joy, the powerhouse, and the motivation behind everything I do.

CONTENTS

ACKNOWLEDGEMENTS

I give the highest praise to God, for with Him, nothing is impossible. He has proven again that once He spoke it, it will come to pass, and once He purposed it, it will happen! If it takes a village to raise a child, I agree with Hillary Clinton that it also takes a village to write a book. I'm eternally grateful to many who contributed to sharpening and shaping me in the prophetic and bringing this book to fruition.

A big thank you to my precious family for your support, strength, and prayer, especially my witty and astute sister Allison, who has been my personal prophet and extraordinaire personal assistant. May you receive blessings upon blessings!

I'm blessed to have the best of friends in my life who have embraced my ministry and gifting with their endless support and love. Thank you, Malika Stephens, Rosalita Singh, Thiadi Rodrigues, Alvina Basdeo-Mohamed, George Clifford, Kofi Stephens, Thandi Fortune, Donna Hamilton, and Benjamin Hooper. You have been my biggest cheerleaders and supporters. You guys are awesome!

A special thank you to my editors Jarienn James and Omeyana Hamilton-Dummett, for your diligence and editing acumen. Special thanks to Rev. Joan Ward; you have been gracious to proofread my raw manuscript and shared invaluable insights and ideas.

A big thank you to my brother from another mother, Harrison Forde. I honor the anointing God has placed on your life for artistic design and creativity and for producing the greatest cover design I could ever imagine.

Thank you, Dr. Walton and the team at Greatness Publishing, for seeing the potential in this manuscript and publishing it.

I salute, honor and celebrate the great men and women God has used over the years that have imparted, impacted, invested, mentored, counseled, corrected, and spoke into my life. Thank you Apostle Eulalee King- Bals, for your obedience to the heavenly call to return to your homeland and raise up prophetic voices. You saw deep wells on the inside of me and brought it out. May God reward you richly!

Thanks to Apostle James Duncan and Prophetess Donna Duncan for your labor and years of bringing the apostolic/prophetic teams to Guyana yearly. It was not in vain. The seeds sown have now turned into a harvest. May the double portion blessing rest on your household continually!

Thanks to Rev. Dr. Deodat Singh for your wisdom and guidance, prayers, constant affirmation, and encouragement. God richly bless you!

Thanks to Apostle Curnal Fahie, you have been my coach and drill sergeant throughout this journey. I've been blessed by your grace and humility, extraordinary wisdom, and encouragement. May the Blessings of God overtake your life!

Thank you, Prophetess Nurita Love, for relentlessly contributing to the vision of the prophetic movement in Guyana and for your encouragement to write the vision and make it plain. It surely shall speak. Vision Board Rocks!

A big thank you to the team at Christ Prophetic Academy (Guyana), including Apostle Patrick Miggins, Apostle Rohan Parsan, Sis. Lily Persaud and others. Your contribution to my growth and ministry have been phenomenal.

Special thanks to Prophetess Peggy Medas for being a modern-day Deborah in my life. Your sagacity and motherly counsel have blessed me tremendously. May heaven continue to open over you!

I'm so grateful to the prophetic Company and prayer warriors, including Prophetess Patricia Miggins, Daunne Dublin, Kendria Dalrymple, Kwayon Duncan, Darryl Sandiford, Tricia Campbell, and others. I truly appreciate your love, support, and encouragement. May you increase in prophetic foresight and insight!

A million thanks to all those who have kept me on their prayer list and covered me in prayer, including Minister Claudette Austin, Prophet Calvin Abrams, Roy Bourne, Sis. Leila, Sis. Carol, Br. & Sis. Niamatali, Oswin and Jackie.

I give kudos to all those I have tutored in the prophetic and those who attended the prophetic activation sessions. Your enthusiasm to Covet to Prophesy has been the inspiration behind this book.

Thanks to all those who have supported and sowed into my life and ministry. May God open the book of remembrance and remember you. I speak a prophet's reward over your life. Thank you all!

FOREWORD

I have known Prophet Delon Aaron for more than fourteen years. He is a prophet of the highest integrity, humility, and effervescence. When God spoke to Apostle Eulalee King-Bals and me in the year 2000 to start a prophetic apostolic move in Guyana, we did not know the persons God would have raised up in Guyana for national and international acclaim.

Prophet Delon Aaron is a prophet to the nations. Although young physically, he is prophetically mature and, over the years, has grown to become the principal of the prophetic school we started in Guyana. Thus, his book is a compilation of his growth in wisdom, knowledge, and experience in the prophetic realm. He shares from a wise and practical standpoint how a person can be activated in the prophetic river of God. As one of the experienced leading prophetic voices in Guyana and the Caribbean, he has recorded gems that you will not find in a lot of prophetic manuals in this book.

As you read this book, you will realize that the prophetic flow is simple and not mystified, and as long as you are filled with the Holy Ghost, the prophetic is in you, and you can be activated to prophesy.

I am amazed to see the phenomenal growth and accuracy in his life, his simplicity, and how God uses him profoundly to minister to the simplest individuals and those in the high echelons of the hierarchy of the church, business, political and social realm. He is an example of those that God spoke to like Jeremiah - "Before I formed thee in the belly I knew thee, and before thou camest forth out of the womb I sanctified thee, and I ordained thee a prophet unto the nations." Jeremiah 1:5

Prophet Delon's integrity is impeccable, and he embodies one of the cornerstone principles of Christ Prophetic Academy worldwide - we do not prophesy for money. As you read this book, you will prophesy. He reveals ways of how God speaks, ways that you can sense when God is revealing the word, ways you can feel and hear the revelation of the word of the Lord and how to articulate, demystify and bring it with simplicity and clarity.

Regardless of whether you are an intellectual genius or not intellectually inclined but have a love and a passion to prophesy, you will. I'm encouraging you to read this book, practice the principles in it, and share it with as many persons as you know because this book is like a treasure chest. You will discover the treasures of the prophetic that will cause you as a beginner to prophesy and as a seasoned prophet, apostle, or prophetic disciple to receive treasures that will encourage, challenge, and cause you to grow in prophetic wisdom and demonstration.

This is a must-read for people interested in the prophetic and who know something about it, but it is also a tool for teaching, activating, and growing in the prophetic. We are in the world that was created by the voice of God, and He wants all of us to prophesy as believers in the Lord Jesus Christ. Prophet Delon is one of those God has raised up as an accurate prophet, teacher, and activator of His prophetic treasures, which lay in our earthen vessel.

This book will have tremendous success not only now but in times to come, even as a reference for prophetic/apostolic schools. I bless you all as you read, study, operate with what you read, and share it widely. Covet to prophesy, and you will. God's blessings and shalom!

Apostle James Duncan
Christ Church International & Global Harvest Apostolic Prophetic Networks,
Brooklyn, NY
Author of PUSH – Prophesy Until Something Happens

ENDORSEMENTS

We are excited to endorse this great and insightful book that will give the reader and student of the prophetic a profound foundation to build on. It opens the realm of the prophetic beyond personal prophecy.

I, Eulalee King Bals, had the privilege not only to identify Delon Aaron's gift and call but to work with him, train, and mentor him. He is a next-generation voice speaking from Guyana to Nations.

Apostles Gerhard Bals and Eulalee King Bals
International House of Apostolic Reformation
Letmathe /Germany

Delon Aaron has been passionate about the ministry of the prophet and the prophetic. The fact that he has written this book is a testament to his commitment for the Body of Christ to come into the understanding of the ministry of the prophet and walking in the prophetic. He has a wealth of knowledge and experience in this area of ministry. He possesses the ability to teach, impart and activate with such simplicity, yet very profound. This book would truly cause an acceleration and explosion in many lives and churches.

Apostle Elsworth Williams
& Prophetess Carmen Williams
Heavenly Light World Outreach Fellowship, Guyana

Prophet Delon Aaron is called by God, anointed, and carries the mantle of the prophetic office. The flow, grace, and relevance that he brings to the ministry is a testimony of a man who hears from God and boldly presents his wisdom with clarity.

The anointing that flowed from his pen through the pages of this book is both fresh and rich. His scholarly approach provides both impartation and inspiration. This book will stir, activate, train , and release you to hear God for yourself.

A must-read book for our generation on how to activate and release the prophetic anointing. I assure you that even if you are not a believer in the prophetic, you will become a believer by the time you finish reading this book.

Rev. Dr. Deodat Singh
The Wesleyan Church, Guyana

Prophet Delon, like David, is a man after God's heart to honor and please him in all he does. His commitment, discipline, and obedience are to be applauded. His service in the office of the Prophet should be emulated. Because of this book, prophets who have stayed dormant due to fear will rise up and take the fight to the enemy's camp.

Every eyeball and ear that gains access to this book will react and be obedient to pick up their mantle and speak the heart of God for this time. God will cause this book to become a catalyst for the body of Christ to Covet to Prophesy. I look forward to reading the other books which will be written by this author.

Rev. Joan Ward
Prophetic Favour & Deliverance Ministires, Barbados
Author of SOAR – Believe, you can live your dream

Sometimes it takes a while to recognize that someone has a special ability to get us to believe in ourselves, to tie that belief to our highest ideals and faith in what God says, and to imagine that together we can do great things. In those rare moments, when such a person comes along, we need to put aside our plans and reach for what we know is possible. Caroline Kennedy

Prophet Delon Aaron is that person. I give my complete endorsement of this book and Prophet Delon himself. This book is a great tool to have in your arsenal as we engage in this continued battle of spiritual warfare.

Prophetess Nurita De Sane-Love,
Senior Pastor Christ Church International Inc,
The Bronx, New York

INTRODUCTION

"Wherefore, brethren, covet to prophesy, and forbid not to speak with tongues."

1 Corinthians 14:39

There are too many voices causing hysteria in the world. Many are claiming to speak for God, but they are not authorized by God. In these times of uncertainty, it is critical for God's authorized voices in each nation to arise, articulate His mind, and bring clear direction.

Prophets bring insight into matters and issues, reveal destiny, and give heaven's counsel. The prophetic gives warnings and shares the secret thoughts of God needed to advance the kingdom. God desires that all may prophesy. Numbers 11:29 *"And Moses said unto them, enviest thou for my sake? Would God that all the Lord's people were prophets, and that the Lord would put his spirit upon them".*

I believe your life is getting ready to change as God activates and releases His prophetic nature in you. My prayer is that as you read this book, you will have a fresh revelation and encounter with the God of the prophetic so that you will grow in your relationship with Him and become one of His authorized voices in the earth.

In the opening verse in 1 Corinthians 14, Paul encouraged us to *"follow after charity, desire spiritual gifts, but rather that ye may prophesy." 1 Corinthians. 14:1*. We also noticed in verse 3 where He explained the purpose of prophecy as edification, exhortation, and comfort. *"But he that prophesieth speaketh unto men to edification, exhortation, and comfort."* He then concludes the chapter encouraging us to *"Covet to prophesy."*

The word "Covet", derived from the Greek word Zeloo means to have warmth feeling for[1]. In other words, it means to be zealous for something or have a strong desire. The majority of the times we see the word Covet being used in the Bible, we are admonished not to do it. The tenth commandment forbids us from coveting what belongs to our neighbour. However, of all the gifts given to the body of Christ, Paul in 1 Corinthians 14 urged the believers to Covet to Prophesy.[2]

In order for us to minister effectively, we have to cultivate that desire to prophesy. If we do not have that desire, we may easily justify our excuses for neglecting the exercise of our gifts. But when we covet to prophesy, our desire becomes stronger than our excuses, our ministry is fulfilled, and people are blessed. This is why Paul encouraged in 1 Timothy 4:14 that Timothy *"Neglect not the gift that is in thee, which was given thee by prophecy."*

Prophecy edifies - Edify comes from the Greek word "okidome," which means edifice or building[3] – a primary purpose in exercising our spiritual gifts is for the building up of the body of Christ. When we prophesy, we build up the believers in their faith and in the things of God. Even though prophecy is one of the most widely used gifts, it is also one of the most misused and abused. Many have been hurt and destroyed in the name of prophecy, but God's intention is that prophecy builds up.

Prophecy brings exhortation, which stirs and encourages believers in their walk with God and in the things of God that advance the Kingdom. We are exhorted to be faithful in service and giving. We are exhorted to worship, pray and study the word of God.

Prophecy also comforts the believers. Believers experience hardships, battles, trials, and testings that not only challenge their faith but can also bring discouragement and depression. What a comfort it is to receive a word that God cares and that He is working it out for our good and that this too shall pass.

This book is not designed to make you a prophet or teach you how to prophesy but rather to activate and stir up that which is already in you. All are not called to be prophets, but all can prophesy. May you receive an impartation that will empower and equip you to speak as one that will bring the clear direction and answers that many are seeking as you allow God to use you. The church is looking to you. The nations are waiting on you. All creation is groaning for you. Heaven is excited about you. God is rooting for you. It's time to Prophesy!

Prophet after God's Own Heart

By Delon Aaron

I have called you a prophet after my own heart

I have ordained, sanctified and set you apart

To fulfill a noble task.

As you walk in the mantle of a renowned art

Through the realms of the supernatural,

I will unfold my heart

You will prophesy, declare, decree, and impart

The feelings, intentions, and thoughts of my heart.

To a people, nation and body that I have birthed

Arise and Speak as an oracle of truth

For I've called you a prophet after my own heart.

CHAPTER ONE

The Prophetic God

"And I fell at his feet to worship him. And he said unto me, See thou do it not: I am thy fellowservant, and of thy brethren that have the testimony of Jesus: worship God: for the testimony of Jesus is the spirit of prophecy."

Revelation 19:10

We serve a God who is Prophetic. He knows the end from the beginning. He is Omniscient - All-knowing. He lives and operates in the prophetic realm. Everything He does is prophetic. He was prophetic at the beginning of creation. He said, let there be, and there was. He spoke, and things came into being. Hebrews 11:3 states that *"... the worlds were framed by the word of God, so that things which are seen were not made of things which do appear."* Nothing happens unless His word is released. Psalm 33:6 *"By the word of the LORD were the heavens made; and all the host of them by the breath of his."*

This same God birthed prophetic children. The prophetic is in our DNA. He formed man out of the dust, breathed into him, and he became a living soul. When He saw that it was not good for man to be alone, He put him to sleep, took a rib out of him, and made woman. God then gave man the prophetic ability by allowing him to exercise dominion in the naming of the woman and animals. Adam was entrusted with that authority of whatever he called it or named it, it is so! David asked the question in Psalm 8:4, *"What is man, that thou art mindful of him? and the son of man, that thou visitest him?"* God saw it fit to be mindful of man in that whatever man purposed it to be, so it was.

God prophesied to Abraham and told him at the age of one hundred years old, that he would have a son with his wife Sarah, who was ninety years old. Sarah laughed when she heard because she was already advanced in age and did not understand His word cannot return to Him void and that He also watches over His word to perform it.

> *"And the Lord visited Sarah as he had said, and the Lord did unto Sarah as he had spoken. For Sarah conceived and bare Abraham a son in his old age at the set time of which God had spoken to him."*
>
> Genesis 21:1-2

Issac's birth was the fulfillment of the prophetic word spoken by God to Abraham.

Again, when God wanted to bring forth His son to redeem man, He brought him forth prophetically. He first sent a forerunner, John the Baptist, who was born to Elizabeth, a woman who was past childbearing age. When the prophecy came to her husband, Zechariah, he doubted, and God made him dumb until such time.

Moreover, Elizabeth hid herself after the prophecy came to pass. She, who was barren and stricken in age, was now pregnant.

God then appeared to a young virgin named Mary, who supernaturally conceived after the Holy Ghost came upon her. She then gave birth to Jesus, who was prophesied to be the Saviour of the world. *"…Behold, a virgin shall conceive and bear a son, and shall call His name Immanuel."* Isaiah. 7:14

> *"But when the fullness of the time was come, God sent forth his son, made of a woman."*
>
> Galatians 4:4

Thus, the Word became flesh, and we beheld His Glory.
In Luke chapter 4, we read how Jesus went into the synagogue and read the prophetic word of prophet Isaiah, *"The spirit of the Lord is upon me, because he hath anointed me to preach the gospel to the poor, he hath sent me to heal the brokenhearted, to preach deliverance to the captives, and recovering of sight to the blind, to set at liberty them that bruised, to preach the acceptable year of the Lord. Afterwards, he closed the book and said to them, "This day is this scripture fulfilled in your ears."* Luke 4:18-20

After he had fulfilled his assignment on earth and cried, it is finished, Paul tells us in Ephesians 4:8-13 *"…he ascended on high and give gifts unto men. And he gave some apostles, some prophets, and some evangelists; and some pastors and teachers. For the perfecting of the saints, for the work of the ministry and for the edifying of the body of Christ, Till we all come in the unity of the faith, and of the knowledge of the Son of God, unto a perfect man, unto the measure of the stature of the fullness of Christ."*

Again, on the day of Pentecost in Acts chapter 2, when suddenly there was a sound from heaven, and they began to speak with other tongues as the Spirit gave utterance and while many were amazed and marveled, some began to mock and said they were drunk with wine. But Peter stood up and declared, *"This is that which was spoken by the prophet Joel."* The prophet Joel had prophesied in Joel 2:28-29 *"And it shall come to pass afterward, that I will pour out my spirit upon all flesh; and your sons and your daughters shall prophesy, your old men shall dream dreams, your young men shall see visions: And also upon the servants and upon the handmaids in those days will I pour out my spirit."*

God is prophetic, and He created mankind in His image and likeness. It is, therefore, natural that He desires and wills that His children speak and create through speech. Like every good Father, He extends this aspect of Himself to us and wishes to have us imitate Him and replicate. He knows all things and shares the secret things with His children, who choose to embrace the prophetic gift.

CHAPTER TWO

The Role of Prophecy

"Surely the Lord God will do nothing, but he revealeth his secret unto his servants the prophets."

Amos 3:7

God wants His voice to be heard. He will not do anything on earth, in your life or nation, without unveiling His plans to His servants through prophecy.

Genesis 18:17 *"And the Lord said, Shall I hide from Abraham that thing which I do*; Sometimes it is not only in our preaching, teaching and evangelizing that we do great exploits. When we look back over the course of history, we can see the prophetic was key in God's people doing great exploits for Him. He used various means and used His prophets in various ways to prophesy.

"For the prophecy came not in old time by the will of man: but holy men of God spake as they were moved by the Holy Ghost."

2 Peter. 1:21

Prophecy is defined as simply communicating the heart, mind, and will of God for His people. The ability to prophesy is not only a special grace and precious gift from God but also an important vehicle for him in revealing His desires and plans for us. That is why Paul exhorted us to desire the ability to prophesy. Paul was encouraging us to put a high priority on prophesying.

There are blessings and benefits of the prophetic not only central to the church but also to us fulfilling our purpose on earth beyond the four walls of it. Often, the prophetic is perceived to be relevant only for the church, but when God speaks, He speaks to individuals, He speaks to families, He speaks to the church, He speaks to governments, and He speaks to nations.

In biblical times, before godly Kings went to war they would seek out a prophet for revelation and direction on what the Lord was saying.

> *"And Jehoshaphat said, Is there not here a prophet of the* Lord *besides, that we might enquire of him?"*
>
> 1 Kings 22:7

When kings had dreams and needed interpretation and their magicians, soothsayers and psychics could not shed light on it, there was always a prophet who came and brought heaven's mind, counsel and interpretation.

> *"And Pharaoh said unto Joseph, I have dreamed a dream, and there is none that can interpret it: and I have heard say of thee, that thou canst understand a dream to interpret it. And Joseph*

answered Pharaoh, saying, It is not in me: God shall give Pharaoh
an answer of peace."

Genesis 41:15-16

"The king answered and said to Daniel, whose name was
Belteshazzar, Art thou able to make known unto me the dream
which I have seen, and the interpretation thereof? Daniel
answered in the presence of the king, and said, The secret which
the king hath demanded cannot the wise men, the astrologers,
the magicians, the soothsayers, shew unto the king; But there is
a God in heaven that revealeth secrets, and maketh known to
the king Nebuchadnezzar what shall be in the latter days. Thy
dream, and the visions of thy head upon thy bed, are these."

Daniel 2:26-28

In 2 Kings 6:8-12 when the enemy's army was plotting and strategizing there was a prophet speaking into the ears of the King, exposing the plans of the enemy and giving Israel an advantage in the battle.

"Then the King of Syria warred against Israel, and took counsel
with his servants, saying, in such and such a place shall be my
camp. And the man of God sent unto the king of Israel, saying,
Beware that thou pass not such a place; for thither the Syrians
are come down. And the king of Israel sent to the place which
the man of God told him and warned him of, and saved himself
there, not once nor twice. Therefore the heart of the king of Syria
was sore troubled for this thing; and he called his servants, and
said unto them, Will ye not shew me which of us is for the King
of Israel? And one of his servants said, None my lord, O king: but

Elisha, the prophet that is in Israel, telleth the king of Israel the words that thou speakest in thy bedchamber."

2 Kings 6:8-12

When God's people were in bondage and they cried out to Him, He delivered them by a prophet. The prophetic brought deliverance and preservation of a nation.

"And by a prophet the Lord brought Israel out of Egypt, and by a prophet was he preserved."

Hosea 12:13

Again, when the Israelites were in Babylonian captivity, Daniel, through prayer, engaged heaven in relation to the prophetic word spoken by Jeremiah and wrought deliverance for His people.

"In the first year of his reign I Daniel understood by books the number of the years, whereof the word of the Lord *came to Jeremiah the prophet, that he would accomplish seventy years in the desolations of Jerusalem. And I set my face unto the Lord God, to seek by prayer and supplications, with fasting, and sackcloth, and ashes."*

Daniel 9:2-3

Prophecy stirred the people to rebuild the temple and also caused them to experience prosperity.

"And the elders of the Jews builded, and they prospered through the prophesying of Haggai the prophet and Zechariah the

son of Iddo. And they builded, and finished it, according to the commandment of the God of Israel, and according to the commandment of Cyrus, and Darius, and Artaxerxes king of Persia."

Ezra 6:14

We also see the prophetic reactivating the dead and reversing a hopeless situation in Ezekiel.

"And he said unto me, Son of man, can these bones live? And I answered, O Lord God, thou knowest. Again he said unto me, Prophesy upon these bones, and say unto them, O ye dry bones, hear the word of the Lord...So I prophesied as I was commanded: and as I prophesied, there was a noise, and behold a shaking, and the bones came together, bone to his bone... Then said he unto me, Prophesy unto the wind, prophesy, son of man, and say to the wind, Thus saith the Lord God; Come from the four winds, O breath, and breathe upon these slain, that they may live. So I prophesied as he commanded me, and the breath came into them, and they lived, and stood up upon their feet, an exceeding great army. Then he said unto me, Son of man, these bones are the whole house of Israel: behold, they say, Our bones are dried, and our hope is lost: we are cut off for our parts."

Ezekiel 37:3-11

Prophecy also brings confirmation and direction that enables us to fulfill God's divine call on our lives. David being anointed as king of Israel by the prophet Samuel demonstrates this.

"And the Lord *said unto Samuel, How long wilt thou mourn for Saul, seeing I have rejected him from reigning over Israel? Fill thine horn with oil, and go, I will send thee to Jesse the Bethlehemite: for I have provided me a king among his sons."*

1 Samuel 16:1

"And he sent, and brought him in. Now he was ruddy, and withal of a beautiful countenance, and goodly to look to. And the Lord *said, Arise, anoint him: for this is he."*

1 Samuel 16:12

The release of prophecy over our lives can change seasons and cycles of frustration and fruitlessness, bringing us into God's divine timing of breakthrough and miracles.

"And the woman conceived, and bare a son at that season that Elisha had said unto her, according to the time of life."

2 Kings 4:17

The role of prophecy cannot be dismissed if we are to see the manifestation of what God has written in the script of eternity concerning us. It was said of Jesus; he came in the volume of the book written of him (Hebrews 10:7). David noted that all the days appointed to him (David) were written in God's book as noted in Psalm 139:16.

We are living in challenging and exciting times. It is vital that God's voice be heard and the intentions of his mind be revealed through prophecy. Destinies hang in the balance until God's will is revealed. As we *Covet to Prophesy*, we will see God's visitation and heaven's manifestation in amazing ways.

CHAPTER THREE

Demystifying the Prophetic

"And the Spirit of the Lord *will come upon thee, and thou shalt prophesy with them, and shalt be turned into another man."*

1 Samuel 10:6

There is a thin line between the prophetic and the pathetic, as well as revelation and divination[4]. The enemy always has a counterfeit of what God has established. We have been witnessing an increase in psychics and the pathetic, who profess to hear from God but are turning ministry into performance. This has caused confusion, paranoia, fear, and ridiculing of the ministry.

One time, I was invited to minister at another church. On entering the building, I felt a tense atmosphere as if the people were skittish. In discussion with the Pastor, he indicated that the leadership had warned them that the prophet was coming, so they needed to get their lives in order. They had the expectation and fear that the prophet was coming to expose everyone's sin.

The prophetic ministry is delicate, and its misuse has brought controversy, misunderstandings, and misconceptions over the years. Thus, many who are called to be prophets are apprehensive about stepping into their gifting. In this chapter, I seek to demystify those notions about the prophetic and bring appreciation to what God has blessed the body with.

Jesus was accused of being an agent of Beelzebub. *"And the scribes which came down from Jerusalem said, He hath Beelzebub, and by the prince of the devils casteth he out devils."* Mark 3:22. He walked on water and they thought he was a ghost. *"And when the disciples saw him walking on the sea, they were troubled, saying, It is a spirit; and they cried out for fear."* Matthew 14:26. When one's prophetic radar is awakened, and he or she begins to hear, sense, and see things in the spirit, it can be overwhelming and scary. Sometimes even the dreams and visions we have can make us feel different. We may think we are weird, strange, or spooky, but it is simply God bringing us into awareness of our calling.

Jesus began to prophesy to his disciples about his crucifixion and the many things he would suffer. Peter readily shut him down, perhaps thinking he was crazy. Jesus' response was insightful. *"But he turned, and said unto Peter, Get thee behind me, Satan: thou art an offence unto me: for thou savourest not the things that be of God, but those that be of men."* Matthew 16:23. Jesus recognized the spirit behind it and rebuked it. The enemy will always attempt to have us question the call on our lives or use others to discount and deny it.

We also saw when God began to awaken Samuel to his prophetic call. He perceived it was Eli who was calling him because he hadn't yet discerned the voice of God. I could imagine Samuel questioning himself, wondering if he was "hearing things." Thankfully, Eli was able to assure him that it was God who was speaking to him.

In the following chapters, I will be sharing more on the ways in which God speaks to us. So if you still have doubts about whether you are hearing from God, you will have greater clarity and recognize His prophetic DNA inside of you.

The impressions and promptings in your spirit that you have been experiencing do not make you a weirdo or strange. In fact, those will be normal experiences on your prophetic journey. For example, sometimes, as you encounter people, you can literally feel their burden and pain. I recall an interesting experience I had while on a ministry assignment to the prisons where I was a part of a group that went to distribute Bibles and minister to the inmates. Entering the compound, my nostrils were permeated spiritually with the putrid scent of death. I've never had such an experience before, and I told a colleague I smell death in this place. We completed our assignment, and two weeks later, my attention was drawn to breaking news on the television - a riot and jail break was happening. Unfortunately, seventeen prisoners died because they were unable to free them from their cells in time.

We cannot afford to dismiss the seemingly strange sensings in our spirit. It is normal for prophetic people to experience these. You may not have the terminology for what you're sensing as yet but do not be quick to trivialize or dismiss it. The prophets tasted death in the pot.

2 Kings 4:39-40, *"And one went out into the field to gather herbs, and found a wild vine, and gathered thereof wild gourds his lap full, and came, and shred them into the pot of pottage: for they knew them not. So they poured out for the men to eat. And it came to pass, as they were eating of the pottage, that they cried out, and said, O thou man of God, there is death in the pot. And they could not eat thereof."*

You might also become the target for mockery like disciples on the day of Pentecost who were perceived to be drunk with wine. *"And they were all amazed, and were in doubt, saying one to another, What meaneth this? Others mocking said, These men are full of new wine."* Acts 2:12-13. Peter, therefore debunked that notion and clarified that what was happening was actually the manifestation of the prophetic word given by the prophet Joel in Acts 2:14-18 *"But Peter, standing up with the eleven, lifted up his voice and said unto them, Ye men of Judaea, and all ye that dwell at Jerusalem, be this known unto you, and hearken to my words; For these are not drunken, as ye suppose, seeing it is but the third hour of the day. But this is that which was spoken by the prophet Joel; And it shall come to pass in the last days saith God, I will pour out my Spirit upon all flesh: and your sons and your daughters shall prophesy, and your young men shall see visions, and your old men shall dream dreams; And on my servants and on my handmaidens I will pour out in those days of my Spirit; and they shall prophesy."*

Sometimes the environment we are emerging from can also cause us to question the prophetic call on our lives. In my own experience, coming from a church that did not emphasize or embrace the prophetic fully was one of the challenges I faced coming forth in my calling and anointing. I was encouraged as I reflected on the life of John the Baptist. The Bible tells us that John was a voice crying in the wilderness. He was the lone voice. He was not polished, neither was his message politically correct. His lifestyle and way of dressing did not fit with the status quo. We are told he ate locust and wild honey and his clothes were camel's hair, yet he was a voice. (Matthew 3:4) Sometimes God will have us be that one voice in that wilderness place, charting the course for others, blazing the trail so they can arise in their calling. In retrospect, I am grateful I did not change churches quickly. The prophetic gift has now been endorsed, and there is room for it to be exercised. I've also seen many others coming forth and flowing in their prophetic gifting and being celebrated. Sometimes not all of us are called to an already established territory. Some of us have to break the ground and pioneer for others. The prophetic anointing is a forerunner's anointing. At the time of Samuel's birth, there was no prophetic in operation, but he was able to shift the atmosphere and cultivate a culture for the prophetic so that others could have emerged and flow in that call. [5] " *And the child Samuel ministered unto the* Lord *before Eli. And the word of the* Lord *was precious in those days; there was no open vision.*" 1 Samuel 3:1

> "*And it was so, that when he had turned his back to go from Samuel, God gave him another heart: and all those signs came to pass that day. And when they came thither to the hill, behold, a company of prophets met him; and the Spirit of God came upon him, and he prophesied among them.*"
>
> 1 Samuel 10:9-10

When we arise in our prophetic call, we are able to partner with heaven to release whatever heaven wants to release in this timeline. The prophetic enables us to function in our kingly anointing and fulfill this partnership. Ephesians 2:6 reminds us, *"And hath raised us up together, and made us sit together in heavenly places in Christ..."* For too long, we have heard the voice of the naysayers, the voice of doom, the voice of the deceivers, the voice of confusion, but God wants the true prophetic voice that brings revelation, direction, confirmation, clarity, counsel, wisdom, edification and truth to come forth.

In teaching the prophetic, we always emphasize that the lack of training can cause persons to dismiss another person's prophetic anointing. As alluded to earlier, the church has seen many theatrics in the name of the prophetic that has caused many to shut it down, despise it and deny it.

It takes faith to embrace the prophetic. *"And he did not many mighty works there because of their unbelief. "* (Matthew 13:58). That's why Mary's response was "be it unto me according to thy word," after receiving the prophecy from the angel Gabriel. *"And Mary said, Behold the handmaid of the Lord; be it unto me according to thy word. And the angel departed from her."* Luke 1:38 At the moment she agreed with the prophetic word, heaven was releasing to her, and she became pregnant with destiny.

Yes, persons may even be offended, but you have to reject being painted with the brush of crazy, weirdo, fanatic, and pathetic. Heaven is birthing forth something great in you, and hell is trembling because of what you are carrying. Oftentimes it may be beyond our articulation and eloquence but do not allow others to define and confine you. The roar of the lion of Judah will put a thunder in your voice that will shake and overthrow demonic systems in the realm of the spirit. You are not speaking gibberish, and neither are you "hearing things". You are hearing what the Spirit is saying. Your words carry weight and authority. Release it and prophesy!:

Jeremiah 1:8-10 declares, *"Be not afraid of their faces: for I am with thee to deliver thee, saith the* Lord. *Then the* Lord *put forth his hand, and touched my mouth. And the* Lord *said unto me, Behold, I have put my words in thy mouth. See, I have this day set thee over the nations and over the kingdoms, to root out, and to pull down, and to destroy, and to throw down, to build, and to plant."*

We are reminded that Satan is the accuser of the brethren, and we're not ignorant of his devices. Thus, if he can accuse what is true and authentic and label it crazy and weird to prevent people from coming into the truth - he will. A true prophetic voice heralds the truth, which sets men free from the lies and deception of the enemy. A true prophetic voice is God's ordained mouthpiece and oracle.

The prophetic call on your life will attract attacks on your reputation and character. However, you must ensure your spirit and mind are guarded. Be obedient, humble, and quick to forgive. When you prophesy, you are a threat to the kingdom of darkness. You destroy demonic principalities and powers and free people from bondages and religious systems. When King Ahab saw the prophet Elijah, he asked him if he was the disrupter. *"And it came to pass, when Ahab saw Elijah, that Ahab said unto him, Art thou he that troubleth Israel? And he answered, I have not troubled Israel; but thou, and thy father's house, in that ye have forsaken the commandments of the* Lord, *and thou hast followed Baalim."* 1 Kings 18:17-18

You are not crazy and powerless! You are God's ordained and authorized voice. Religion, the traditions of men, and the legalistic "letter of the law" cannot kill and silence what God has put in you. Despite the rejection attributable to ignorance and man's ill-conceived opinions, I say to you Prophesy! There is a river in your belly. Out of your belly shall flow rivers of living waters (John 7:38). Arise and prophesy!

Also, we must always remember that God did not commission us into the prophetic ministry to be popular. At times our message may not mesh with the status quo. But like Elijah, we may have to endure rejection. At times we may be like Micaiah, the one in four hundred that is not going soothsay with the masses to appease the king.

> *"And the king of Israel said unto Jehoshaphat, There is yet one man, Micaiah the son of Imlah, by whom we may enquire of the* Lord: *but I hate him; for he doth not prophesy good concerning me, but evil. And Jehoshaphat said, Let not the king say so."*
>
> 1 Kings 22:8

Prophetic ministry is not a social media platform for the likes and applause of men. Your prophetic word should be sound in the word and uttered according to God's heart. As prophets, we are dealing with many critics and skeptics of the prophetic. But do not allow the accusation and intimidation of the enemy to cause you to curtail your gifting or compromise the truth. Truth is the foundation of sound, prophetic ministry.

> *"And the messenger that was gone to call Micaiah spake unto him, saying, Behold now, the words of the prophets declare good unto the king with one mouth: let thy word, I pray thee, be like the word of one of them, and speak that which is good. And Micaiah said, As the* Lord *liveth, what the* Lord *saith unto me, that will I speak."*
>
> 1 Kings 22:13 -14

I believe in the days to come, we will begin to see an emerging of new prophetic voices as God invades religious systems and denominations that have shut down and excluded the prophetic. These voices may not be known, but they will arise. They may not be popular or the favorite, but they will have the backing of heaven.

These are the days God is causing His spirit to come on ordinary men and women, transforming them into powerhouses. They will shift atmospheres and regions through their prophecies. Saul was transformed in a prophetic atmosphere and began to prophesy. The people asked, *"Is Saul now a prophet?"* (1 Samuel. 19:24). It was strange for many to fathom Saul prophesying. God can use anyone. He even used a donkey to prophesy, so He can most certainly use you too. Open your mouth and prophesy!

There is an indictment against the church because we have permitted all kinds of craziness and called it prophetic because we did not want to offend. In some cases, the prophetic was utilized only as a marketing tool to attract sowers and givers to the ministries. This can be likened to strange fire that God judged Aaron's sons for in Leviticus 10:1-2, *"And Nadab and Abihu, the sons of Aaron, took either of them his censer, and put fire therein, and put incense thereon, and offered strange fire before the Lord, which he commanded them not. And there went out fire from the Lord, and devoured them, and they died before the Lord."* Not all prophets have to get into violent convolutions and theatrical performances to release a word. Even though the prophetic is known for spontaneity, one does not need to be a lunatic. Yes, it may be a word of correction or rebuke, but we cannot tolerate dishonor to the ministry and give credibility to things done out of order. If we encourage such, then we're allowing the spirit of the wild ass, loose cannons, renegades, fanatics and hirelings to create havoc in the body of Christ.

Moreover, we cannot divorce character from the calling. Often, the foolishness we witness is due to the absence of maturity and character in the prophet and zeal without wisdom.

God is interested in the character of his prophets more than their gifting. We cannot claim to represent God as his mouthpiece and do not exhibit his characteristics of holiness, righteousness, truth, and trustworthiness. Many have become victims of what is known as the Integrity Deficiency Syndrome (IDS) as a result of compromise, dubious and unethical dealings. We saw this happen with Elisha's servant Gehazi who, after Elisha had healed Naman and was being offered gifts by Naman, refused to accept such from him. However, Gehazi subsequently went after Naman and lied to him to receive the gifts that Elisha refused.

"But Gehazi, the servant of Elisha the man of God, said, Behold, my master hath spared Naaman this Syrian, in not receiving at his hands that which he brought: but, as the Lord *liveth, I will run after him, and take somewhat of him. So Gehazi followed after Naaman. And when Naaman saw him running after him, he lighted down from the chariot to meet him, and said, Is all well? And he said, All is well. My master hath sent me, saying, Behold, even now there be come to me from mount Ephraim two young men of the sons of the prophets: give them, I pray thee, a talent of silver, and two changes of garments. And Naaman said, Be content, take two talents. And he urged him, and bound two talents of silver in two bags, with two changes of garments, and laid them upon two of his servants; and they bare them before him. And when he came to the tower, he took them from their hand, and bestowed them in the house: and he let the men go, and they departed. But he went in, and stood before his master. And Elisha said unto him, Whence comest thou, Gehazi? And he said, Thy servant went no whither. And he said unto him, Went not mine heart with thee, when the man turned again from his chariot to meet thee? Is it a time to receive money, and to receive garments, and oliveyards, and vineyards, and sheep, and oxen, and menservants, and maidservants? The leprosy therefore of Naaman shall cleave unto thee, and unto thy seed for ever. And he went out from his presence a leper as white as snow."*

2 Kings 5:20-27

This was the same Gehazi that Elisha had prayed that the Lord open his eyes in 2 Kings 6:17 *"And Elisha prayed, and said, LORD, I pray thee, open his eyes, that he may see. And the LORD opened the eyes of the young man; and he saw: and, behold, the mountain was full of horses and chariots and horses of fire round about Elisha."* Elisha had received a double portion anointing from Elijah. That double portion anointing should have been transferred to Gehazi, but unfortunately, due to Gehazi's character flaws he could not receive the impartation of that anointing. The Bible records Elisha died and that anointing was in his grave and was activated when a dead man was inadvertently dropped on Elisha's bones and came back to life in 2 Kings 13:20-21.

> *"And Elisha died, and they buried him. And the bands of the Moabites invaded the land at the coming in of the year. And it came to pass, as they were burying a man, that, behold, they spied a band of men; and they cast the man into the sepulchre of Elisha: and when the man was let down, and touched the bones of Elisha, he revived, and stood up on his feet."*

God hates deception and dishonesty; that's why Jesus declared in Matthew 7:22-23. *"Many will say to me in that day, Lord, Lord, have we not prophesied in thy name? and in thy name have cast out devils? and in thy name done many wonderful works? And then will I profess unto them, I never knew you: depart from me, ye that work iniquity."*

The prophetic is a gift that character has to be of utmost importance since any hint of deficiency can blemish one's ministry and ultimately contribute to their destruction and downfall.

Further, it can also result from pride, lack of submission to leadership, lack of mentorship, protocol, and training in most instances. Accountability is necessary because of the nature of the prophetic ministry and the risk of destruction to lives. It is time that we reject the madness masquerading as the prophetic.

The culture and times seemingly require us to reject those voices that cry *prepare the way of the lord*. But it is not how loud one sounds or how much noise one makes that denotes the level of anointing on their life. Prophecy is not only a sound but also the very breath of God being released. We need to discern the authentic sound of God coming forth in the prophecy. Paul encouraged us in 1 Thessalonians 5:20-21, *"Despise not prophesying, prove all things; hold fast that which is good."* Proving all things means that even when it comes to the prophetic, the word of God should be the foundation and litmus test to establish the truth of what is being spoken.

Many in Noah's days presumed him to be crazy for building an ark and forecasting rain. Moreover, Isaiah prophesied that a virgin would give birth to a baby, something that was and is still medically impossible. We cannot allow the finite minds of men to define the things of the Holy Spirit. Jesus said to Nicodemus, *"Whatsoever is born of the flesh is flesh and whatever is born of the spirit is spirit."* John 3:6

This is why it's important for prophecy to be judged. *"Let the prophets speak two or three, and let the other judge."* 1 Corinthians. 14:29. God will not have us do anything that is contrary to His word. His word is forever settled. All prophecies must be judged based on the word of God. Many bad practices have attracted attention and have not brought glory to God. But we cannot throw out the baby with the bath water. The prophetic was given by God, and it still has an important role in the kingdom.

When Moses was asked to stop others from prophesying in Numbers 11:29, he stated, God's desire is that all may prophesy. "And Moses said unto him, Enviest thou for my sake? Would God that all the Lord's people were prophets, and that the Lord would put his spirit upon them!" Paul posits in 1 Corinthians. 14:31 that "you can all prophesy." "For ye may all prophesy one by one, that all may learn, and all may be comforted." Although you may be able to give a prophetic word, that does not make you a prophet. There are different levels of the prophetic.

For example, the first level is the spirit of prophecy, which any believer can operate in when the atmosphere is charged in Revelation 19:10 *"And I fell at his feet to worship him. And he said unto me, See thou do it not; I am thy fellowservant, and of they brethren that have the testimony of Jesus: worship God: for the testimony of Jesus is the spirit of prophecy."*

The second level is the gift of prophecy which is one of the manifestations of the Holy Spirit and this can be resident in a believer. *"To another the working of miracles; to another prophecy; to another discerning of spirits; to another divers kinds of tongues; to another the interpretation of tongues."* 1 Corinthians12:10

The third level is the office of the prophet which is a fivefold ministry office, and you must be called and set in (ordained to) this office. *"And he gave some, apostles; and some prophets; and some, evangelists; and some, pastors and teachers."* Ephesians. 4:11

"And God hath set some in the church, first apostles, secondarily prophets, thridly teachers, after that miracles, then gifts of healings, helps, governments, diversities of tongues."

1 Corinthians. 12:28

We cannot put God in a box. God allowed Joseph to prophesy in prison. He was able to interpret Pharaoh's baker and butler's dreams (Genesis 40: 9-21). The prophet Jeremiah suffered much persecution for the prophecies he gave, including imprisonment. Although he got into trouble for the word, he cried out and likened it to fire in his bones that he could not contain.

"Then I said, I will not make mention of him, nor speak any more in his name. But his word was in mine heart as a burning fire shut up in my bones, and I was weary with forbearing, and I could not stay."

Jeremiah 20:9

When God called Moses as His authorized voice to confront Pharaoh to let his people go, Moses complained and sought to excuse himself out of that assignment.

"And Moses said unto God, Who am I, that I should go unto Pharaoh, and that I should bring forth the children of Israel out of Egypt?"

Exodus 3:11

"And Moses said unto the Lord, O my Lord, I am not eloquent, neither heretofore, nor since thou hast spoken unto thy servant: but I am slow of speech, and of a slow tongue."

Exodus 4:10

Moses felt unqualified. Nevertheless, as God reassured Moses, he submitted to the call, and God was able to use him to deliver an entire nation out of bondage. Hosea 12:13

God can use whoever and whatever to deliver His word and His people. He used David, a simple shepherd boy with a slingshot, to defeat the Giant Goliath and deliver His people. *"So David prevailed over the Philistine with a sling and with a stone, and smote the Philistine, and slew him; but there was no sword in the hand of David."* 1 Samuel 17:50

He also used Gideon, who was from the weakest clan, and he was also the least among his family. *"And he said unto him, Oh my Lord, wherewith shall I save Israel? Behold, my family is poor in Manasseh, and I am the least in my father's house. And the* Lord *said unto him, Surely I will be with thee, and thou shalt smite the Midianites as one man."* Judges 6:15-17

God sometimes gives instructions which are contrary to conventional wisdom. Gideon was instructed to reduce the size of his army from three thousand to three hundred. *"And the LORD said unto Gideon, By the three hundred men that lapped will I save you, and deliver the Midianites into thine hand: and let all the other people go every man unto his place."* Judges 7:7

Another instant of adhering to God's unconventional ways lies in David refusing to wear Saul's amour to fight Goliath. *"And David girded his sword upon his armour, and he assayed to go; for he had not proved it. And David said unto Saul, I cannot go with these; for I have not proved them. And David put them off him."* 1 Samuel 17:39

We cannot allow the doubters and deniers to stop and hinder us from fulfilling the mandate we have been given. I know sometimes you may feel like Gideon; you are the least among the brethren, or like Jeremiah, you cannot speak. You may even be fed up and frustrated because you do not understand what is happening or why you are not being recognized. There may not be a reference point in your generation or fellowship, but it does not matter. God still called you and will use you. If He can use a donkey to utter His word, He can surely use you! *"And the* Lord *opened the mouth of the ass, and she said unto Balaam, What have I done unto thee, that thou hast smitten me these three times?"* Numbers 22:28

CHAPTER FOUR

Hearing in the Spirit

"Blessed is the man that heareth me, watching daily at my gates, waiting at the post of my doors."

Proverbs 8:34

Part of our orientation into the prophetic is the ability to recognize and hear God's voice. There are many voices on earth. God speaks, but other voices are drowning him out. *"For God speaketh once, yea twice, yet man perceiveth it not."* Job 33:14 We need to pay attention to the voices that have our attention and make every effort to let God's voice be dominant in our lives.

In 1 Kings Chapter 19, Elijah was instructed by God to stand by the mountain. There was a wind, an earthquake, a fire but after that, a still small voice. *"And after the earthquake a fire; but the Lord was not in the fire: and after the fire a still small voice."* 1 Kings 19:12. God can speak in a still small voice like a lamb or He can speak with the roar of the lion[6] as was declared in Joel 3:16 -*"The Lord also shall roar out of Zion, and utter his voice from Jerusalem; and the heavens and the earth shall shake: but the Lord will be the hope of his people, and the strength of the children of Israel."*

When we can clearly recognize God's voice, it enables us to walk in His promises and blessings. The inability to hear God's voice often leaves us frustrated, overwhelmed, anxious, in despair, and desperate and may cause us, like Saul, to even seek out an unauthorized voice. Saul consulted a witch, which was never God's will for him. This is also not God's intention for us. God commanded the children of Israel to "suffer not a witch to live" (Exodus 22:18). This is because a witch pretends to hear from God but is a medium for the devil.

The Hebrew word for prophecy, "nabi," comes from the root word "naba," which means to bubble up or gush forth. True prophecy bubbles up and gushes forth. John 7:38 announces that *"...out of your belly shall flow rivers of living waters."* On the other hand, false prophets, psychics, witchcraft workers presume to hear from God by consulting familiar spirits and thereby have to cook up and conjure up revelations.[7]

God wants us to hear his voice not only for ourselves but also for others so we can become oracles of his truth. When we are hearing so many different *"Thus saith the Lord,"* we witness confusion in the body. We can only know and recognize his voice if we spend time in God's presence. Jesus said, "my sheep know my voice and the voice of a stranger they will not obey" (John 10:27). Spending quality time in prayer, fasting, and the word sharpens our hearing in the spirit. Samuel had to learn to hear God's voice so that he would not mistake it for that of Eli.

When we covet to prophesy, it means we desire to know and hear God's voice and be empowered to announce what he's saying. This is the ability to hear in the spirit. We see in 1 Kings 18:41-46 when there was a drought, the prophet Elijah was able to tap into the frequency of the spirit and heard a sound of abundance of rain. He heard in the spirit what did not reflect what was happening in the natural. But as he continued to press in the spirit, on the mountain, he was able to send his servant to go and look because he heard a sound. He sent his servant up several times to check, but it was only on the seventh time that he noticed something which in his assumption was not significant. It was a little cloud, the size of the palm of a man's hand. However, this was the confirmation that Elijah was waiting for. Thereafter, he told his servant to hasten and tell King Ahab to prepare the chariots because an abundance of rain was coming.

When we begin to engage the prophetic God, we will hear in our spirit what the Lord is saying to us, others, the church, and the nations. You will be praying for someone, and you will hear clearly God's direction for their life. You will be in your time of worship and devotion, and the Spirit will speak to you. You may be in your time of fasting or reading the word, and His voice will be loud and clear. You will hear Him speaking to you concerning your future and that of your household, you will hear Him speaking to you about your marriage, your business, your career, your ministry, and you will hear Him speaking to you concerning your nation and many other things.

In 2 Kings, the prophet Elisha heard clearly in the spirit that in twenty-four hours, things were going to shift. At that time, there was an economic crisis in the nation.

"Then Elisha said, Hear ye the word of the Lord; *Thus saith the* Lord, *Tomorrow about this time shall a measure of fine flour be sold for a shekel, and two measures of barley for a shekel, in the gate of Samaria. Then a lord on whose hand the king leaned answered the man of God, and said, Behold, if the* Lord *would make windows in heaven, might this thing be? And he said, Behold, thou shalt see it with thine eyes, but shalt not eat thereof. And there were four leprous men at the entering in of the gate: and they said one to another, Why sit we here until we die? If we say, We will enter into the city, then the famine is in the city, and we shall die there: and if we sit still here, we die also. Now therefore come, and let us fall unto the host of the Syrians: if they save us alive, we shall live; and if they kill us, we shall but die. And they rose up in the twilight, to go unto the camp of the Syrians: and when they were come to the uttermost part of the camp of Syria, behold, there was no man there. For the* Lord *had made the host of the Syrians to hear a noise of chariots, and a noise of horses, even the noise of a great host: and they said one to another, Lo, the king of Israel hath hired against us the kings of the Hittites, and the kings of the Egyptians, to come upon us. Wherefore they arose and fled in the twilight, and left their tents, and their horses, and their asses, even the camp as it was, and fled for their life."*

2 Kings 7:1-7

In this story, four lepers were outside the city at the gate. They were rejected because of the stigma attached to that condition. It is interesting to note that they had no access to the King, prophet, or prophecy. They were excluded, isolated and exiled because of their situation but what they did not hear with their natural ears, they heard with their spiritual ears. Even though these lepers were on the outside, they had an ear to hear on the inside what God said He was going to do. And thus God put a word in their spirit, and when they heard they got up and said one to the other why sit ye here and die?

When we *Covet to Prophesy,* we will never be in a place where we die for lack of hearing from God. Because there is a desire and zeal to prophesy, there will be a flow and release of revelation. It is as simple as the law of supply and demand. And since there is a demand, it necessitates a posture and positioning in one's spirit to hear. This positioning will allow us to be transformed into conduits of God's voice and enable us to easily discern whether the voices competing for our ears have been authorized with credentials from heaven to speak on its behalf.

CHAPTER FIVE

Seeing in the Spirit

"Moreover the word of the Lord *came unto me, saying, Jeremiah, what seest thou? And I said, I see a rod of an almond tree."*

Jeremiah 1:11

Our spiritual eyes were created to see in the realm of the spirit. When God was confirming Jeremiah's prophetic mandate on his life, He did so by engaging his spiritual eyes. Two times in Jeremiah chapter one, the Lord asked him, "what seest thou?" Jeremiah then described what he saw, and then God began to articulate the meaning of what Jeremiah had seen.

The ability to see in the spirit is one of the earliest confirmations of having a prophetic gift because, in times past, a prophet was called a seer (I Samuel 1:9). The word seer comes from the Hebrew word "ro'eh or ra'ah, meaning one who sees.[8]

When we Covet to Prophesy, it activates not only the seer anointing but also the revelatory gift of the word of knowledge in us. This was also consistent with Jesus' ministry. In John chapter one, Philip invites Nathaniel to meet Jesus, and Nathaniel questions whether any good thing can come out of Nazareth. When Nathaniel arrives Jesus comments about Nathaniel saying "behold an Israelite indeed, in whom there is no guile" (John 1:46). Nathaniel marvelled at the insight Jesus had into his character and inquired how Jesus had known him. Jesus responds in John 1:48 saying "...*before Philip called thee, when thou wast under the fig tree, I saw thee.*" Nathaniel then had a revelation of who Jesus was and confirmed he was the son of God.

Further, we note in John 1:50-51, Jesus said unto Nathaniel, "...*Because I said unto thee, I saw thee under the fig tree, believest thou? Thou shalt see greater things than these.* "*Verily, verily I say unto you, hereafter ye shall see heaven open, and angels of God ascending and descending upon the son of man.*"

Jesus was activating Nathaniel as a seer. Jesus noted that Nathaniel would move and function in an anointing to see in a greater dimension. Heaven will open up to him, and he will see greater things, including angelic activities. This anointing would cause his spiritual sight to be so heightened that the supernatural would be a common experience for him. God also desires that you see into the spiritual realm.

It is a great injustice against the prophetic ministry when we see it downgraded to impressing people about seeing their bank account numbers and house lots etc. Seeing in the spirit enables us to see greater things. John encountered one such thing in Revelation 4.

"After this I looked, and, behold, a door was opened in heaven: and the first voice which I heard was as it were of a trumpet talking with me; which said, Come up hither, and I will shew thee things which must be hereafter. And immediately I was in the spirit: and, behold, a throne was set in heaven, and one sat on the throne."

Revelation 4:1-2

It is important to note that John said he was in the spirit. For us to see in the spirit, we have to be in the spirit. Paul in Romans 8:14 reminds us *"for as many as are led by the Spirit of God, they are the sons of God".* It is my conviction that God desires that those who He is raising up to speak as His oracle be in the Spirit so they can clearly articulate His heart and mind. This cannot be done from the flesh. When we operate in the flesh, we operate in that which is natural and does not allow for revelation. Jesus said to Peter in Matthew 16:17, "Flesh and blood could not reveal this to you." Operating in the spirit is moving in the realm that is uncommon. It is the realm where your prophesying will not be by personal might or power but by the Spirit. It is the realm where your prophesying will not be through your imagination or the personal details you are familiar with about a person's life. Paul tells us in 1 Corinthians 14:25 that when prophecy is in operation and unbelievers come into the service, the secrets of hearts will be made known, and they will fall down and worship and proclaim that God is true.

I believe we can only see the greater if we ascend to the place where downloads and revelations are given. Jesus told Nathaniel heaven will open up unto him. When you Covet to Prophesy, heaven will open up unto you. You will walk into places and see angelic activities. When Elisha prayed, God opened his servant's eyes, and he was able to see those who were with them were more than those against them. He could not have seen this with his natural eyes.

> *"And Elisha prayed, and said,* Lord, *I pray thee, open his eyes, that he may see. And the* Lord *opened the eyes of the young man; and he saw: and, behold, the mountain was full of horses and chariots of fire round about Elisha."*
>
> 2 Kings 6:17

Jesus said to Nicodemus that which is born of the flesh is flesh and that which is of the spirit is spirit (John 3:6). We must dwell in the spirit to move in revelation and not information. While information may be head knowledge i.e. what we are aware of as fact or truth, revelation requires faith that leads to conviction. This was the dilemma Nicodemus faced as he interacted with Jesus. The information he knew and understood brought limitation to his faith, thus he could not fathom a man being born again outside of his mother's womb.

God wants us to come out from the familiar realm where we are just seeing things in the natural and begin to live in the third dimension where we will have discernment, foresight and insight. In the familiar realm, we can see with the natural eyes. However, when we ascend to the third dimension, God causes us to see the invisible realm as Elisha did in 2 Kings 16.

Mark records the account of Jesus healing the man that was blind by spitting in his eyes. At first, he said he could only see men as trees, but after Jesus placed his hands upon his eyes again, he was able to declare, "I can see clearly now."

> *"And he looked up, and said, I see men as trees walking. After that he put his hands again upon his eyes, and made him look up: and he was restored, and saw every man clearly."*
>
> Mark 8:24-25

Seeing men as trees is not normal. Jesus was developing his sight in the realm of the spirit. He was moving him from one dimension to another. In most cases, when Jesus performed miracles, they were instantaneous, but, here this man's sight was being restored in stages. This was a natural progression in the healing of the man's sight. Likewise, we grow in stages in the prophetic and develop our spiritual sense of sight and discernment. Jesus was healing this blind man in stages. The process was not yet finished and thus he needed a second touch and what was blurred came into sharp focus. Now he was able to differentiate men from trees. He who was blind then saw clearly. It does not matter what stage you are at in seeing in the spirit. As you seek God for a fresh touch and greater clarity, He will cause your eyes to be opened to see greater in the realm of the spirit.

I pray that as you press into the spirit, the portal of heaven will be unlocked over you, and you will have revelation and insight and that God will begin to show you things concerning your assignment and purpose. May He show you details concerning his plans for your life. May He remove nightmares and give you dreams, visions, and encounters as you press into the spirit. In the words of one of my apostolic fathers, Apostle Patrick Miggins, May God spit in your eyes!

CHAPTER SIX

Sensing in the Spirit

"But strong meat belongeth to them that are of full age, even those who by reason of use have their senses exercised to discern both good and evil."

Hebrews 5:14

The God we serve is one of diversity and creativity and thus, there is no exclusive way in how he speaks to us. Even though the dominant ways God speaks to us might be through our spiritual senses of hearing and seeing, He also speaks through our other senses of tasting, touching, and smelling. As we progress in the prophetic, we must learn how to access these dimensions in order to function effectively in our ministry. In Hebrews 5:14 we are reminded that by reason of use, we sharpen these senses. One of the manifestations of the Holy Spirit is the discerning of spirits. Therefore, we can discern through our spiritual senses. Whilst pursuing my studies in counseling, my tutor said to us, "The hallmark of counseling is listening with our bodies because oftentimes a person may not say much as you engage them." Likewise, tapping into our prophetic senses helps us to listen with our bodies to what the Holy Spirit is impressing upon us.

The basis of the prophetic ministry is revelation. God can reveal things to us by giving us impressions, nudges and feelings in our body where we have an inward knowing or sensing about someone or something. We can literally pick up things such as sensations or impressions in certain areas of our body where God might want us to become aware of a person's pain for example. We can have impressions in our emotions where we feel led to minister to persons in a specific direction. God can also give us promptings, illuminations, and perceptions of things in the spirit. This was illustrated in Acts 14, where Paul, while preaching at Lystra, healed an impotent man.[9]

> *"And there sat a certain man at Lystra, impotent in his feet, being a cripple from his mother's womb, who never had walked: The same heard Paul speak: who steadfastly beholding him, and perceiving that he had faith to be healed, Said with a loud voice, Stand upright on thy feet. And he leaped and walked."*
>
> Acts 14:8-10

We also saw in Acts 16 where the young lady who was under the spirit of divination was following Paul and Silas. Paul became grieved in his spirit by her utterances and cast that spirit out of her. Even though her statements were true, Paul sensed the presence of an evil demonic spirit in her.

"And it came to pass, as we went to prayer, a certain damsel possessed with a spirit of divination met us, which brought her masters much gain by soothsaying: The same followed Paul and us, and cried, saying, These men are the servants of the most high God, which shew unto us the way of salvation. And this did she many days. But Paul, being grieved, turned and said to the spirit, I command thee in the name of Jesus Christ to come out of her. And he came out the same hour."

Acts 16:16-18

We also note Peter's encounter with Simon the sorcerer in Acts 8:23, where he said, *"For I perceive that thou art in the gall of bitterness, and in the bond of iniquity."*

Sometimes we can walk into a place or environment and sense the spirits that are in operation. On prayer walks around the neighborhood, I sense the prevailing spirits in certain homes. When visiting churches, you can sense whether the Holy Spirit is or is not in operation. You can also pick up tension in the atmosphere. Whilst ministering to certain individuals, you can sense and smell unclean spirits.

We see in 2 Kings 4:40 the men tasted death in the pot while in Revelation 10:10 after the angel gave John the book which he ate and it tasted like sweet honey, but soon after he had eaten it, it was bitter in his belly. Things we consume that cause our stomach to be bitter are spewed out. Thus, the angel told John to prophesy to nations. The word of God is sweet, and so his prophetic unction was to release or spew out and make known what God had put in him to the nations.[10]

"And I went unto the angel, and said unto him, Give me the little book. And he said unto me, Take it, and eat it up; and it shall make thy belly bitter, but it shall be in thy mouth sweet as honey. And I took the little book out of the angel's hand, and ate it up; and it was in my mouth sweet as honey: and as soon as I had eaten it, my belly was bitter. And he said unto me, Thou must prophesy again before many peoples, and nations, and tongues, and kings."

Revelation. 10:9-10

When we *Covet to Prophesy*, it allows us to navigate realms of possibilities in the spirit that God communicates with his people.

CHAPTER SEVEN

Speaking Prophetically

"...The word is nigh thee, even in thy mouth, and in thy heart:
that is, the word of faith, which we preach..."

Romans 10:8

One of the ways we activate and demonstrate the supernatural dimension of the prophetic ministry is through the power of our voice. The words that we speak are not abstract ordinary words, but the Spirit breathed word which is anointed and released with potent creative power to pull manifestation from the realms of the spirit. God spoke, and the world came into being. In Genesis 1:3 He said, let there be, and there was. Psalm 29:4 *"The voice of the Lord is powerful,"* and Proverbs 18:21 tells us, *"Death and life are in the power of the tongue."*

Every born-again believer who is filled with the Holy Ghost already speaks in the dimension of the supernatural when we flow in the language of the spirit. Prophesying is simply activating that dimension to manifest through our speech. Paul declared in Romans 4:17 what should generally be our stance to *"call those things as not as though they were."* Jesus said in Mark 11:23, *"if we say to this mountain…"* We are not expected to just stand and watch the mountain but open up our mouth and speak to it. There is great power in speaking.

When we *Covet to Prophesy*, we are going into the realm of not only speaking prophetically but also supernaturally. That is why when a prophetic word is released, things shift and align. Ezekiel chapter 37 records the dialogue God had with the prophet regarding dry bones. The scene was a graveyard, a place of no return and of the dead. Where there was no prospect for life or hope of a future, God commanded the prophet to prophesy to the dry bones in Ezekiel 37:4 *"Again he said unto me, Prophesy upon these bones, and say unto them, O ye dry bones, hear the word of the* Lord." Ezekiel spoke to the dry bones and let them know I have heard from God and I have a word from God. It's not over for you dry bones. God has not forgotten you dry bones. I know in the natural there's no sign life can ever come again, but dry bones hear the word of the Lord I'm declaring over you dry bones – you shall live!

It is important to note that Ezekiel did not say hear "my" words but the word of the Lord. When we prophesy, it is the word of the Lord that we are releasing and not man's opinion. God's word is not only divinely inspired and anointed but also has authority when it is released. Isaiah 55:11 tells us His word will not return void unto Him but shall accomplish that which He pleases. Thus, Ezekiel spoke the word of God, and the dry bones responded. Situations, things, and elements can respond when we instruct them by speaking prophetically, and that which seemed impossible becomes possible.

Joshua commanded the sun and moon in Joshua 10:12 to stand still, and they obeyed.

> *"Now unto him that is able to do exceeding abundantly above all that we ask or think, according to the power that worketh in us."*
>
> Ephesians. 3:20

Further, we are not constrained to prophesy to individuals. We can also speak prophetically over nations and over governments. We can speak over the church and over families. We can speak over our marriages and over our pregnancies. We can speak over the economy and over businesses, etc. The word brings revelation and insight and replaces darkness and ignorance. It brings order where there is chaos and confusion. It builds up that which was torn down and breaks up that which is not in God's plan. It confirms callings and anointing. It strengthens and prepares us for the return of Christ. The prophetic word is a seed that births life and new things. The prophetic word is from the Hebrew word "dabar," meaning it has the potential to push us forward and accelerate us into destiny. The prophetic word literally comes behind us and pushes us forward because it comes with the backing of heaven. Thus, when a prophetic word is released over our life, we are catapulted into a new season and cycle.

CHAPTER EIGHT

Enemies of the Prophetic

"Despise not prophesyings. Prove all things; hold fast that which is good."

1 Thessalonians. 5:20-21

Again, while the prophetic is one of the most controversial and misunderstood ministries, it is also one of the most important ministries given to the church by God. The prophetic ministry exposes the works of the enemy, and this makes it a target for attacks and assaults. Anything that makes people aware of God's blueprint for their lives will be subjected to attacks from the adversary.

When the prophecy came that Jesus would be born King of the Jews, it infuriated Herod to go after the male babies. When the children of Israel increased and multiplied because of the prophetic word God had spoken over Abraham, that his descendants will be numerous, the king of Egypt ordered the midwives to kill the male babies. Herod had John the Baptist thrown in prison and his head cut off for condemning his marriage to his wife, who was previously married to his brother.

> *"For Herod had laid hold on John, and bound him, and put him in prison for Herodias' sake, his brother Philip's wife. For John said unto him, It is not lawful for thee to have her. For John said unto him, It is not lawful for thee to have her."*
>
> Matthew 14: 3-4

Jesus released a prophetic word to his disciples that they are going over to the other side in Mark 4:35 and soon after a severe and terrifying storm arose.

> *"And the same day, when the even was come, he saith unto them, Let us pass over unto the other side. And when they had sent away the multitude, they took him even as he was in the ship. And there were also with him other little ships. And there arose a great storm of wind, and the waves beat into the ship, so that it was now full."*
>
> Mark 4:35-37

The forces and spirits that are against the prophetic can be vicious, brutal, and cruel. They all have one assignment – release a spirit of murder to kill what God has birthed or desires to live.

The enemy has no idea of God's intention and plans for your life until a prophetic word is spoken over you. When he becomes knowledgeable, he initiates outright warfare to block, stop and hinder you from coming into manifestation. That's why Paul encourages us to war a good warfare over the prophecies concerning you.

"This charge I commit unto thee, son Timothy, according to the prophecies which went before on thee, that thou by them mightest war a good warfare;" 1 Timothy 1:18

In this chapter, I'll be addressing four spirits which I encountered during my prophetic journey.

1. Jezebel

Jezebel is a spiritual assassin spirit that the enemy unleashes against the prophets. This spirit thrives where leadership is weak and uses seduction, rejection, and intimidation as its weapon. This spirit seeks to hijack the prophetic ministry by having a parallel false prophetic. It was this spirit that issued a death warrant on Elijah's life and brought depression. It was also this spirit that carried out a massacre on the prophetic and had prophets hiding in the cave.

> *"And Ahab told Jezebel all that Elijah had done, and withal how he had slain all the prophets with the sword. Then Jezebel sent a messenger unto Elijah, saying, So let the gods do to me, and more also, if I make not thy life as the life of one of them by tomorrow about this time. And when he saw that, he arose, and went for his life, and came to Beersheba, which belongeth to Judah, and left his servant there. But he himself went a day's journey into the wilderness, and came and sat down under a*

juniper tree: and he requested for himself that he might die; and said, It is enough; now, O Lord, take away my life; for I am not better than my fathers."

1 Kings 19:1-4

Many have the prophetic gifting and anointing but are hiding in caves because of Jezebel attempts on their lives. The spirit of Jezebel challenges the loyalty and allegiance of the prophets. It is important to note that this spirit can operate through any gender. [11]

2. Religion

Religion is another anti-prophetic spirit that uses powerful, gangster, mafia structures to keep people in bondage by legalistic and traditional means. Its main agenda is to kill the prophetic. This spirit can be easily overlooked because we tend to believe everything with a spiritual overtone is of God. Because this spirit is strongly legalistic, it makes no room or provision for the prophetic. The religious spirit operates as if it is God's sole vessel with authority to hear and convey His message. Anyone who dares to question the authority will be suppressed without hesitation. The religious spirit twins with the spirit of pride and can be very stubborn and resistant[12].

The religious spirit hates revelation shuts down the things of the spirit. In 2 Corinthians 3:6, Paul said, "The letter kills but the spirit gives life". The religious spirit denies us access to the things of the spirit. When we are limited in revelation, it brings stagnation and ultimately death. The prophetic brings knowledge, revelation and restoration. It builds up, exhorts and comforts the believers. The religious spirit judges and condemns. Negative words are one of the prime instruments used by this spirit. When this spirit is in operation, there is no room for edification or restoration.

This spirit nullifies the anointing and quenches the Holy Spirit. It compromises and twists the truth for error. Paul called them out for having a form of godliness but denying the power thereof.

3. **Fear**

Fear represents a stronghold that kills the prophetic and hinders believers from stepping out into their calling. To flow in the prophetic requires faith. We prophesy according to the measure of our faith.

> *"Having then gifts differing according to the grace that is given to us, whether prophecy, let us prophesy according to the proportion of faith."*
>
> Romans 12:6

Fear paralyzes us because it operates with the spirit of doubt and unbelief and can cause us to question the call of God on our lives and our own ability to come forth as His oracle. We may fear criticism, opposition, rejection, and persecution. Fear also robs us of the joy, passion and zeal needed to flow in our gifting and anointing.

A fear frequently associated with the prophetic is being labeled a false prophet after declaring an incorrect prophecy. This fear prevents many persons from tapping into their gift and call. The prophetic grows and develops in an atmosphere of faith. My spiritual mentor in the prophetic, Apostle Eulalee King-Bals, always encouraged us as prophetic students to declare - *"I can Prophesy!"* This has helped me to overcome my fear and unlocked the prophetic unction in me. When we overcome the spirit of fear, we operate in the boldness and confidence necessary to prophesy.

God reminds us in Isaiah 41:10, *"Fear thou not; for I am with thee: be not dismayed; for I am thy God: I will strengthen thee; yea, I will help thee; yea I will uphold thee with the right hand of my righteousness."* Paul also reminds us, *"For God has not given us a spirit of fear, but of power, and of love, and of a sound mind."* 2 Timothy 1:7

4. Witchcraft

Witchcraft is an enemy of the prophetic because it is an affront and counterfeit to the true prophetic ministry. This spirit operates in the soulish realm, is highly demonic, manipulating, controlling, and uses divination and sorcery to kill destiny. Many can unknowingly operate in this spirit, releasing charismatic prayers and prophecies over persons that are nothing but curses and judgments. In Exodus 7:11-12, "Then Pharaoh also called the wise men and the sorcerers: now the magicians of Egypt, they also did in like manner with their enchantments. For they cast down every man his rod, and they became serpents: but Aaron's rod swallowed up their rods." when Aaron's rod transformed into a serpent, Pharaoh called his magicians, and with their enchantments, their rods also turned into serpents. This spirit is subtly infiltrating the prophetic where we are seeing a lot of commercializing and merchandizing of the anointing. As mentioned earlier, in 1 Samuel 28:8 when Saul could not hear from God, he reverted to consulting a witch. God hates this spirit. *"And Saul disguised himself and put on other rainment, and he went, and two men with him, and they came to the woman by night: and he said, I pray thee, divine unto me by the familiar spirit, and bring me him up, whom I shall name unto thee."*

"Suffer not a witch to live."

Exodus 22:18

"For rebellion is as the sin of witchcraft, and stubbornness is as iniquity and idolatry. Because thou hast rejected the word of the Lord, he hath also rejected thee from being king."

1 Samuel 15:23

He stated, witchcraft is likened to rebellion. Rather than seeking the true God for revelation, this spirit presumes to hear from God but actually gets its information from the demonic realm.

The call to the prophetic is a ministry of warfare, and thus we have to be mindful of these enemies to the prophetic. Thus, it behooves those in the prophetic ministry to live a consecrated life that is defined by strong prayer. We have been given power and authority to overcome these enemies, and they must be exposed and confronted.

CHAPTER NINE

Guidelines for Prophesying

"Let all things be done decently and in order"

1 Corinthians. 14:40

God wants to be honored and glorified in all we do. Here are a few guidelines that should be considered when prophesying:

1. Be open to ways God can speak to you. Do not put him in a box by expecting him to speak one way at all times. You can hear the still small voice of the lamb or the roar of the lion.[13]

2. Be willing to step out by faith. Sometimes all it may take is you saying, "And the Lord will say unto you" and He will fill your mouth with the rest.

3. Prophesy in love. This must be the reason we desire to prophesy. God loves you and trusts you with His word. He also loves the person you are ministering to. Keep this in mind always.

4. Stay prayed up and powered up with the spirit. Without the Holy Spirit, our prophecy is mere words.

5. All prophecy must be aligned and judged with the word of God. He cannot contradict Himself.

6. Trust God for the wisdom to turn a negative into a positive. Let your prophecy bring hope and encouragement.

7. Do not prophesy beyond your measure of faith. Stay within your realm. Whether you are operating in the spirit of prophecy, gift of prophecy or the office of a prophet[14]- prophesy according to the measure of your faith.

8. Just because you have a word, it does not mean you have to speak it. Timing is key. Sometimes God may have us interceding and praying for someone instead of sharing with them or others what He showed us.

9. The spirit of the prophet is subject to the prophet (1 Corinthians 14:32). You can control the flow.

10. Declare only what God shows you.

11. Do not use prophecy to flatter.

12. Use wisdom when prophesying publicly about sensitive issues.

13. Do not be quick to expose and prophesy judgment. The desire to prophesy should be to edify, exhort and comfort 1 Corinthians 14:3 states, *"But he that prophesieth speaketh unto men to edification, and exhortation, and comfort".*

14. Be humble.

15. Do not compete with others, especially when prophesying within a presbytery setting or on a team.

16. Submit to leadership.

17. Do not prophesy for money.

18. Guard against the spirits of pride and arrogance

19. Do not neglect training and mentorship. Many have a genuine gift but lack the training and guidance.

20. Not all prophecy has to be predictive. God can speak to our past, present and future.

21. Ensure the prophetic word is recorded so it can be reviewed and referenced.

22. Be yourself because God chose you to deliver the word. He will use your unique voice and way of expression to convey what He is saying. We can emulate others without being a copycat and losing our own personality and uniqueness.

PRAYER TO ACTIVATE THE PROPHETIC IN YOU

"Neglect not the gift that is in thee, which was given thee by prophecy, with the laying on of hands of the presbytery".

1 Timothy. 4:14

Father, in the name of Jesus, I thank you for your plans for my life and ministry. I thank you that right now, You are stirring and awakening the river of the prophetic in me, and You are causing me to hear, sense, see and feel in the Spirit. I thank you that you are giving me clear discernment to speak with clarity and accuracy. I thank you that You are giving me fresh revelation, insight, and understanding in the mysteries of the kingdom. I take authority over the spirits of fear, doubt, unbelief, intimidation, compromise, and that which seeks to limit, confine and restrict me. I bind and rebuke these spirits from operating in my life, and I speak freedom and liberty to prophesy. Father, I believe that according to your word, You are pouring out Your spirit upon all flesh and You are anointing and activating me as a voice to my generation. Let Your divine sentences flow from my lips that I can declare boldly - thus saith the Lord! Father, I thank You for giving me a new confidence, and I pray that heaven will open up and Your glory flows. Let signs, wonders, and demonstrations of Your power manifest. I pray You will unravel hidden and secret things unto me. I pray that You will open doors of favour and opportunity for me to make known Your truth and I thank You for doing it in Jesus' name. Amen!

PROPHETIC DECREES AND DECLARATIONS

"Thou shalt also decree a thing, and it shall be established unto thee: and the light shall shine upon thy ways."

Job 22:28

I decree the Spirit of the Lord is upon me, and He has anointed me to declare the good news of the kingdom.

I decree and declare a new day is dawning upon my life and ministry, and I am anointed with fresh oil and uncommon favour.

I decree my ministry takes off. With Godspeed, I soar in my prophetic destiny.

I decree nations come to my light and kings to the brightness of my rising.

I decree new doors of favour and opportunities are opening for me to exercise my gifting.

I decree and declare I am strong in the Lord and in the power of His might.

I decree and declare I speak with the wisdom of heaven and the words of my mouth are seasoned with grace.

I decree and declare my heart is instructed in the things of the Spirit, and I move in the timing of the Lord, knowing what to, when to do it, and how to do it.

I decree and declare I walk by faith and not by sight, and I see the invisible and hear the inaudible.

I decree and declare the anointing upon my life is relevant and my ministry is recognized, honored, and celebrated.

I decree and declare God is taking my life and ministry to another level.

I decree and declare the Lord establishes the works of my hand and ministry, and I am blessed to be a blessing.

I decree and declare I am instructed of the Lord and the voice of a stranger I do not follow.

I decree and declare God is birthing in me the full measure of His spirit and ministry, and I do undeniably great exploits.

I decree and declare that I am the head and not the tail, and God makes me His everlasting pride and the joy of many generations.

I decree and declare my mouth shall tell of His righteousness and salvation all day.

I decree and declare I shall not die but live to declare His mighty acts to my generation.

I decree and declare the grace of God is heavy upon my life, and His hand is mighty upon me.

I decree and declare the mouth of the Lord has spoken this, and His hand will perform it.

A PROPHETIC WORD FOR YOU

"The lion hath roared, who will not fear? The Lord God hath spoken, who can but prophesy?"

Amos 3:8

For the Lord will say unto you that my call upon your life is sure and these are the days when I am bringing you into a greater awareness and understanding of the things of the Kingdom. And as you ascend to my mountain and walk in a deeper intimacy with me, you will begin to see and hear in the realm of the spirit like never before. And I shall cause your eyes to be opened and your ears to hear and your tongue to be unlocked. Yes, I shall awaken your spiritual senses and that which was dormant in you, and I will unveil My heart and the hidden things unto you. I will expand your capacity for revelation and flood you with dreams and visions. You shall have impressions and promptings of the spirit, and I will expand my gifts and anointing in you, and I will make you like a new wineskin prophet who will not be restricted by tradition or guided by the opinion and ideologies of men. For yes, I have called you, and even like Jeremiah, I put my words in your mouth. Say not that I cannot prophesy and say not that I cannot speak. For in this season, I shall cause you to rise up in power and rise up with boldness to release that which I am stirring in the innermost being of your spirit.

You will begin to prophesy and speak as my mouthpiece. Indeed out of you shall come forth a voice of wisdom and a voice of truth; one that will bring counsel and direction to my church and to many. I shall endow and empower you with my anointing for the supernatural, and many will be blessed, and many will be fed with my word. It will refresh and nourish their souls. I will make known my plans and intentions for their lives - and what I purpose to do. I shall even cause yokes and bondages to be broken off of many. Have not I said my word is like a hammer that breaks, and I will cause heavenly portals to be open up as you prophesy? There will be visitations of angels, and I shall cause a release of rain and release of glory, and my fire will fall. My winds will blow and many will know surely I the God, Yahweh, is speaking and many will experience my presence and power.

My kingdom will be advanced and there will be healing and deliverance and breakthrough and outpourings of my spirit. I shall overturn the agendas of darkness and plots of hell will be exposed and many will come into freedom and liberty. So even as you Covet to Prophesy and embrace that which I have placed upon your life I will make you a sign and a wonder, and many shall know that surely I have called you and surely I am using you and surely I'm gracing you with my prophetic mantle. You will move with new authority and new boldness and new power; for yes, I've called you, and yes, I am raising you to prophesy for such a time as this says the spirit of the Lord.

PROPHETIC ACTIVATIONS

"So I prophesied as I was commanded: and as I prophesied, there was a noise, and behold a shaking, and the bones came together, bone to his bone."

Ezekiel 37:7

Scripture

The prophetic word is released using the wording of the scripture. For example, Psalm 23. And Lord will say unto you because I am your shepherd you shall not want etc.

See a Picture

This exercise activates the seer anointing. Ask the Lord to show you a picture and use it to develop a word for the person. For example, I see a tree, and the Lord will say you will be like a tree planted by the rivers of water etc.

Hear Something

This exercise helps you to prophesy to a person based on what you heard. You can hear a sound and use that to launch into the prophetic word. For example, I hear the sound of a lion roaring, and the Lord will say unto you I am putting a roar in your voice etc.

One Word

Sometimes God can give us one word, and we use that word to develop the prophetic flow. For example, if the Lord gives you the word Restoration - and the Lord will say unto you I am restoring the years that the locust and palmerworm and caterpillar have eaten etc.

Piggyback

This exercise allows a more experienced person to prophesy first, and then another person will follow them in releasing the word to a person based on what jumps out at them, whilst the previous person was prophesying.

Adopted from The Prophet's Manual by John Eckhardt

CONCLUSION

"And Samuel grew, and the Lord was with him, and he did let none of his words fall to the ground."

1 Samuel 3:19

This book came into being as a manifestation of a prophetic word spoken over my life. I could have never imagined myself prophesying much more becoming an author. This is surely a testament and testimony of the faithfulness and greatness of our God and that the prophetic is one of the gifts that can be awakened and stirred up. As Paul said to Timothy *"fan into flame the gift which is within you"* (2 Timothy 1:6). There is an unction and a sure word in you for your generation. Do not neglect it but stir it up. Everyone born of God and filled with the Holy Spirit has the ability to prophesy. I've seen how since being activated in the prophetic has transformed me from an introverted individual to one who God has been taking to nations, training and activating others in the prophetic and speaking His word over great men and women in the Kingdom.

The main emphasis of this book is for you to discover the prophetic DNA in you, activate it and flow in it, so that you can be a blessing to the kingdom. This book was written with those in mind who have been wavering and wrestling with the prophetic call on their life and can also be used as a reference for the beginners and those seasoned in the prophetic.

We are told at the time when Samuel was born, the word of the Lord was rare in those days. (1 Samuel. 3:1) That was a dark time in history. Imagine no one was coming forth with revelation or a word of prophecy. Jesus said "man shall not live on bread alone but by every word that proceeds out of the mouth of God" (Matthew 4:4). God is speaking and there is a rhema word that is proceeding out of His mouth. These are exciting times we are living in as He pours out his spirit upon all flesh so that his sons and daughters can prophesy. It is my passion to see many more arise as prophetic voices and messengers of the rhema word.

> *"For Moses truly said unto the fathers, A prophet shall the Lord your God raise up unto you of your brethren, like unto me; him shall ye hear in all things whatsoever he shall say unto you."*
>
> Acts 3:22

ABOUT THE AUTHOR

Prophet Delon Aaron is an emerging cutting-edge prophetic voice. He is known for his keen accuracy and profound prophetic teaching. He has a strong prophetic mantle for nations and has ministered prophetically throughout Guyana, across the Caribbean and North America. Prophet Delon was mentored and trained in the Prophetic by Apostle Eulalee King-Bals who is based in Germany with her husband, Apostle Gerd Bals. They are the founders of International House of Apostolic Reformation.

Prophet Delon currently serves as Principal of Christ Prophetic Academy (Guyana), a non-denominational mobile prophetic academy that trains and activates persons in the prophetic from various denominations in Guyana. CPA (Guyana) is an affiliate of Christ Prophetic Academy International under the leadership of Apostle James Duncan, Founder and Overseer of Christ Church International, Brooklyn, New York. Prophet Delon is an Accountant and Risk Manager by profession and also the holder of a Distinguished Toastmasters award from Toastmasters International. Prophet Delon resides in Guyana, South America with his beautiful wife Ilene and two sons Zachary and Zion.

Prophet. Counselor. Author.
Delon Aaron

Stay connected
Website: www.delonaaronglobal.com
Email: info@delonaaronglobal.com

ENDNOTES

1   Bible Tools "Dictionary and word search for zeloo (Strong's 2206) http://www.bibletools.com (accessed June 16, 2021)

2   Rodney Francis, It's Time to Prophesy, (accessed December 16, 2019) http://www.gospel.org.nz

3   Bible Hub "Dictionary and word search for okidome (Strong's 3619) http://www.biblehub.com (accessed June 16, 2021)

4   Rick Joyner,The Prophetic Ministry (Morning Star Publications)

5   John Eckhardt, The Prophet's Manual (Charisma House)

6   Rick Joyner, The Prophetic Ministry (Morning Star Publications)

7   Charles Samuenege and Stphen Garner, Essentials of the Prophetic (Rivers Publishing Company)

8   Ibid

9   Ibid

10 Robert Henderson, How to your senses prophetically blog, (accessed June 18, 2021, http://www.destinyimage.com

11 Ryan Lestrange, Hell's Toxic Trio, (Charisma House)

12 Ibid

13 Rick Joyner, The Prophetic Ministry (Morning Star Publications)

14 Charles Samunege and Stephen Garner, Essentials of the Prophetic, (Rivers Publishing Company)

www.ingramcontent.com/pod-product-compliance
Lightning Source LLC
Chambersburg PA
CBHW051546120626
46551CB00013B/1396